History Journeys

# A Victorian Journey

Peter Hepplewhite

HODDER
Wayland

an imprint of Hodder Children's Books

Produced for Hodder Wayland by
Discovery Books Ltd
Unit 3, 37 Watling Street, Leintwardine, Shropshire SY7 0LW, England

First published in 2003 by Hodder Wayland, an imprint of
Hodder Children's Books

British Library Cataloguing in Publication Data
Hepplewhite, Peter
A Victorian journey. - (History journeys)
1. Transportation - Great Britain - History - 19th century -
Juvenile literature 2. Great Britain - History - Victoria,
1837-1901 - Juvenile literature
I. Title
388'.0941'09034

0 7502 3955 7

Printed and bound by G.Canale & C. S.p.A. - Borgaro T.se - Italy

Designer: Ian Winton
Editor: Rebecca Hunter
Illustrations: Mark Bergin

Hodder Children's Books would like to thank the following
for the loan of their material:

**The Bridgeman Art Library**: page 12; **Discovery Picture Library**: page 27 (top);
**Hulton Archive**: *cover*, pages 10, 11, 16, 18, 23; **The Illustrated London News
Picture Library**: page 13; **Mary Evans Picture Library**: pages 5, 7, 8, 9, 14, 15, 17,
19 (both), 20, 21, 22, 24, 25, 26, 27 (bottom), 28, 29 (both).

Hodder Children's Books
A division of Hodder Headline Limited
338 Euston Road
London NW1 3BH

# CONTENTS

# THE RAILWAY AGE

**I**t was September 1851 and ten-year-old Laura Watson was too excited to sleep. Her trunk was packed and tomorrow she was going on holiday. Laura lived in Newcastle-upon-Tyne and was to travel by train with her father and governess to see the Great Exhibition in London. After visiting the city her father had promised they would take a few quiet days by the sea in Brighton.

Queen Victoria reigned from 1837-1901. During her long rule Britain became the leading industrial country in the world and built a huge overseas empire. Historians call this vibrant time the Victorian era. The Victorians were the first high-tech society. They lived in an age of rapid technological change and nothing showed this more than the breathtaking spread of the railways.

(*Right*) The rail network in 1851, the year of Laura's journey. Her route is highlighted.

George Stephenson built the first proper railway from Stockton to Darlington. This opened in 1825 and ran for 43 km (27 miles). It was built to carry coal but ran one, horse-powered, passenger train a day. Before the Stockton-Darlington line was even finished, Stephenson was planning a bolder scheme. In 1830 he completed the first steam passenger railway, from Liverpool to Manchester. In 18 months it carried 700,000 people and made a hefty profit.

George Stephenson was the first great railway engineer. He designed, surveyed and built complete railways, from laying the tracks to manufacturing the locomotives.

Soon a web of railways began to link Britain's major cities and ports. The line from London to Birmingham opened in 1838 and the link to Gateshead, just across the River Tyne from Newcastle, was completed by 1844. When Victoria became queen there were about 1,400 miles (2,300 kilometres) of railway track. When she died this had soared to 20,000 miles (32,000 kilometres).

Most railways around the world are 4 feet 6 inches (1.3 metres) wide. This was the distance between the wheels of coal wagons in the mines of north-east England, where George Stephenson learned his trade. He used the same width on his railway lines and set a standard that most other engineers followed.

# THE INDUSTRIAL REVOLUTION

**T**he following morning Laura woke early, but had to wait patiently for her father. He owned a rope works on the banks of the River Tyne and had gone to see that all was well before he left for London. Newcastle was a thriving city and Mr Watson sold ropes to shipyards and mines across northern England.

The growth of Victorian towns was even more astonishing than the spread of the railways. In 1750 most people lived and worked in the countryside. Over the next 100 years, this traditional lifestyle was turned upside down by a wave of new ideas and inventions. Historians call this the Industrial Revolution.

'Locomotives in every stage of progress meet the eyes on every side. When we reflect that each machine contains more than 5,000 pieces of metal and costs about £2,000 and that one railway company has 500 such machines, can we fail to be impressed?'

A DESCRIPTION OF THE STEPHENSON LOCOMOTIVE WORKS IN NEWCASTLE, 1855.

All over the country small market towns turned into booming centres of industry as factories, ironworks, chemical plants and shipyards were built. Different communities became famous for different products: Manchester for cotton mills and cloth; Sheffield for steel; Stoke-on-Trent for pottery and china; and Birmingham for engineering and metal-working.

THE BRITISH ASSOCIATION AT NEWCASTLE-ON-TYNE—BIRD'S EYE VIEW OF THE CITY
DRAWN BY ROBERT JOBLING

**A bird's eye view of Newcastle in 1889.**

Newcastle became a centre of the coal trade. But by 1851 there were many industries in the city too — brewing, brick making, iron and lead works, shipbuilding, glass making and, of course, locomotive building.

**Many of the products made in Britain were sold abroad and the country became rich – as this advert for a Sheffield firm shows. No wonder the Victorians proudly boasted that they lived in the 'workshop of the world'.**

**CONSTANTINE BROTHERS,**
MERCHANTS, AND MANUFACTURERS OF ALL KINDS OF
**SAWS, FILES, STEEL,**
*Suitable for the United States, Canadian, the British Colonies, and Continental Markets;*
**CALICO WEBS, MACHINE KNIVES, LEDGER BLADES, SPIRAL CUTTERS, &c.,**
68 & 70, HOLLIS CROFT, SHEFFIELD.

Manufacturers of the celebrated Goods marked
C.B
F. CONSTANTINE.
BATTISON & CO.
L. COLBECK.
PORTERS.

The population of most cities soared during the Victorian era, as this table shows:

| City | 1801 | 1851 | 1871 |
|------|------|------|------|
| Birmingham | 71,000 | 233,000 | 344,000 |
| Glasgow | 77,000 | 345,000 | 522,000 |
| Newcastle | 33,000 | 88,000 | 128,000 |
| Manchester | 75,000 | 303,000 | 351,000 |
| London | 959,000 | 2,362,000 | 3,254,000 |

In 1851 the census recorded a momentous change. The population of Britain had reached nearly 21 million. And, for the first time, more than half lived in towns and cities, not the countryside.

# DEADLY TOWNS

**L**aura passed the time, until her father returned, reading with her governess in the nursery. Laura lived in Summerhill, a square of big terraced houses with a private park. She lived a wealthy and privileged life in a comfortable home, with servants to look after her. She knew little of the dirt and squalor in which many poorer people spent their lives.

The one-room home of a London costermonger, a street trader, in 1872.

Industry had brought wealth to some Victorians, but lives of misery to others. The new towns grew so quickly that they were grim places to live. Terraces of cheap houses were built close to factories and workshops. Most had no drains or running water and were often damp and cold.

The streets were not paved and were usually full of rubbish. Factory chimneys belched out filthy smoke, polluting the atmosphere and blocking out the light. Diseases like cholera and typhoid were rife and killed thousands, especially children. Newcastle was well known as one of the most crowded and unhealthy cities in Britain.

'In the sewers of Newcastle, boys from 10 years of age combine amusement and profit by rat catching. One boy will take from four to eight rats and sell them for 2d or 3d (1-1 ¹/₂p) each, according to size. They are bought by persons who resell them at about 6d (2 ¹/₂p) to be worried by dogs!'

MR WILLIAM LEE, INSPECTOR OF THE BOARD OF HEALTH, 1853

In 1851 about 1 million people worked as servants. The most common job for a girl in Newcastle was domestic servant. Victorian servants in the 1850s were poorly paid: housemaids earned £12-£14 a year and cooks £11-£17 a year. This is just over £1 a month. A pair of well-made boots would have cost about 10 shillings, so a servant would have had to save up to afford a pair.

As town centres became over-crowded, richer middle-class families, like Laura's, moved to the outskirts, or suburbs. They lived in detached villas or terraces of large houses with gardens and plenty of fresh air. To run their homes they hired servants: housemaids, nurserymaids, cooks, valets, gardeners and grooms. In the 1850s a man who earned £1,000 a year could easily afford six servants.

**Bedford Park, a wealthy Victorian suburb in 1882.**

# HORSE POWER

**A**t last it was time to go. Tom, the groom, drove the horses and carriage to the front of the house and loaded the trunks. Laura watched her father smiling as they pulled away. He was pleased that he could afford to keep a carriage. 'It impresses the neighbours, shopkeepers and customers, my girl. It shows them we are carriage people.'

Railways caught the imagination of the Victorians, but for everyday transport they relied on horses to pull passengers and goods.

A rich London family in their carriage in 1867.

Wealthy families like Laura's kept a two-horse, four-wheel carriage like a landau or a barouche. But even a one-horse carriage, like a gig, was enough to show the high standing of the owner. In 1856 around 200,000 people kept a private carriage.

**Coaches from Newcastle to Gateshead**

BELSAY.—A coach leaves the Lowther Inn, Newgate St., every Tues.,Thurs., and Sat. at 4 p.m.

BLACKHILL.—A coach leaves the White Swan Inn, Cloth Market, every afternoon at 6.

CONSETT AND LEADGATE.—A coach leaves the White Swan Inn, Cloth Market, every afternoon at 4.

CONSETT.—A coach leaves the White Swan Inn, Cloth Market, every morning at 7.

DIPTON.—A coach leaves the White Swan Inn, Cloth Market, every afternoon at 4.

OTTERBURN.—A coach (carrying the mail bags), leaves the Garrick's Head, Cloth Market, every morning at 7.    Carries no passengers.

PONTELAND.—A van leaves the Phœnix Inn, Newgate Street, Tuesdays, Thursdays, and Saturdays at 4 p.m.

SHOTLEY.—A coach leaves the White Swan Inn, every afternoon at 6.

STAMFORDHAM.—A coach leaves the Victoria Hotel, Newgate Street, every Tuesday, Thursday, and Saturday at 4 p.m.

WHALTON.—A van leaves the Phœnix Inn, Newgate Street, every Tuesday, Thursday, and Saturday at 4 p.m.

WHITTINGTON AND STAMFORDHAM.—A coach leaves the Victoria Hotel, Newgate Street, every Tuesday and Saturday at 4 p.m.

**A coach timetable from *Christie's Directory of Newcastle and Gateshead*, 1874.**

Carrier wagons moved heavy goods and parcels to places the railways did not reach, or to and from stations or ports. Drawn by eight or more horses, depending on the load, they were the heavy goods lorries of their day. The first horse buses — known as omnibuses — were used in London in 1829 and the idea quickly spread to other large towns. There were even traffic jams as city streets became busy with carts delivering everything from coal and ice to milk and bread.

Railways caused a cut in the use of horses for long distance travel but led to an increase in local use. The number of working horses doubled between 1850 and 1902 to 3.5 million. By 1903 London had 4,000 horse buses carrying 500 million people every year.

**This painting, dated 1850, is called *Past and Present Through Victorian Eyes*. It shows the fate of long distance stage-coaches – too slow and expensive to compete with trains.**

# RAILWAY STATIONS

**S**oon they pulled up at the bustling station and Tom went to seek a porter. Laura marvelled at the elegant building, opened only a year ago by Queen Victoria. Soon Tom returned to say the train was waiting at the platform. With the help of a porter, he lifted the trunks on to the roof of a first class carriage, while the others stepped aboard.

This painting, *Paddington Station, London*, by W P Firth shows the excitement and colour of a Victorian station in 1802.

Railway stations fascinated Victorians. They brought people of all classes together — from Dukes to chimney sweeps. Nothing like this had ever happened before! And though the wealthy bought first-class tickets and ordinary people third-class — they would all travel at the same speed.

Large stations were built to impress travellers. The Victorians believed that railways were the greatest achievement of

**Newcastle Central Station was built in the classical style, with a dramatic portico 200 feet (61m) long and 50 feet (15m) wide at the front. But the train shed behind was very modern – the roof had three huge arches of wrought iron and glass, held up by iron pillars. Notice the horse-drawn trams.**

the human mind and wanted to celebrate them in stone, iron and glass. Euston Station, opened in 1837 for the London and Birmingham Railway, set a high standard. It had a huge portico (porch) — like something out of ancient Athens. Even small stations were built with features borrowed from Greek temples or medieval castles.

Inside, stations were as busy as markets. Most had a small army of uniformed staff: porters, ticket clerks and signalmen and a station-master. Alongside the booking-office, waiting-rooms and toilets there might be a hotel, a buffet, a bar, a book stall, a hairdresser and a host of shops.

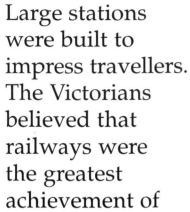

"It appears to me that Rail Roads are the Vulgarest, most injurious to Health of any mode of conveyance [transport]. Mobs of well dressed Ladies and Gentlemen are collected at every station, to examine and pry into every Carriage and the actions of every Traveller."

THE DUKE OF WELLINGTON, 1848

In the 1850s railway carriages still looked like horse-drawn vehicles: stagecoaches with padded seats for first class and plainer wagons with hard wooden seats for third class. The luggage was stored on top and sometimes caught fire if hot ashes blew back from the engine.

13

# BUILDING RAILWAYS

**H**er father smiled at Laura as the train puffed slowly out of the station. 'My dear, you are about to see one of the most impressive views in the world — the River Tyne from Robert Stephenson's High Level Bridge. The great works of our railway engineers take my breath away.' Laura pressed her nose against the window, she didn't want to miss a thing.

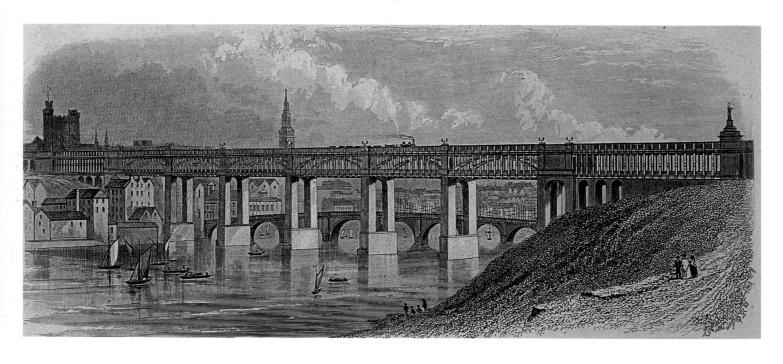

**The High Level Bridge in Newcastle was designed by Robert Stephenson and opened in 1849. It brought the main line from London into the heart of Newcastle. The road and rail decks were made of cast iron.**

Railway engineers were celebrities in the 1850s. Everyone knew the names of men like Robert Stephenson (George's son — and an even better engineer than his dad!) and Isambard Kingdom Brunel. In command of armies of workers called 'navvies', their railway lines ripped through the countryside with great cuttings, viaducts and bridges.

Navvies worked hard, with few machines to help them. Their tools were picks, shovels and wheelbarrows. A good navvy was expected to shovel about 20 tonnes of earth a day.

Brunel was a strong-minded genius who could turn his hand to any engineering task — from steamships to docks. He was only 27 when he was appointed engineer to the Great Western Railway (GWR) and set out to build a new, faster railway — with broad gauge track 7 feet (2.1 metres) instead of 4 feet 6 inches (1.3 metres).

Many of the first railway labourers learned their skills building canals. They were called navigators and got the nickname 'navvies'. By 1847 there were about 255,000 navvies building railways.

He surveyed the line, bargained with landowners to cross their property, designed the tunnels, bridges and stations — and for good measure he drew up the specifications for engines and carriages. By May 1845 the service from London to Exeter was the fastest in the world.

**15**

# TRAVELLING BY TRAIN

**T**he journey to London took over ten hours. The train stopped for a refreshment break at York and Laura's father bought them all hot mutton pies and tea from a platform vendor. The journey went smoothly until they were pulling into Lincoln. Then, the engine broke down and it was an hour before a new locomotive arrived.

Even for first-class passengers a Victorian railway journey could be uncomfortable. Each carriage was divided into compartments but there were no corridors. And no buffet cars — or toilets! The only heating in winter came from foot-warmers — metal flasks filled with hot water. Lighting was very poor, with a single oil lamp in each compartment. Passengers who wanted to read brought their own candles. Trains took long stops at some larger stations so that passengers could buy food and visit the toilet.

**Three classes of travel on the Manchester to Liverpool railway.**

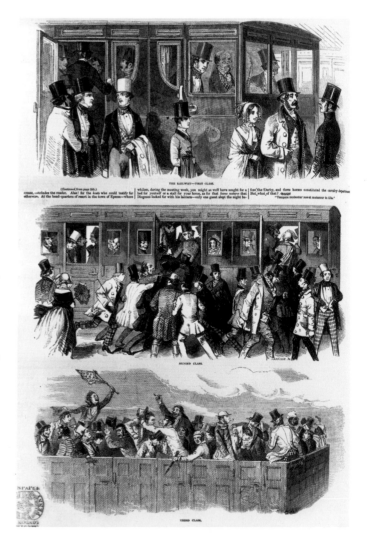

Safety features were slow to improve too. At first, signals had depended upon men stationed along the track waving flags but as the number of lines, points and junctions grew, a better system was needed.

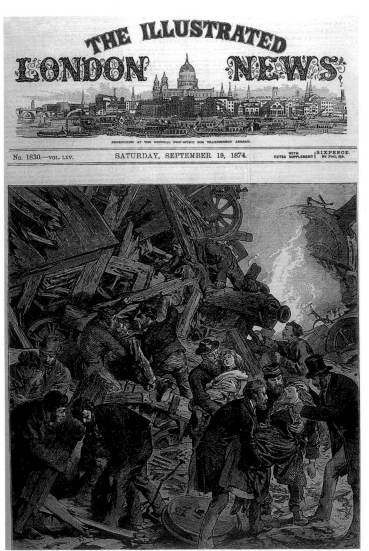

By the 1850s groups of mechanical signals were controlled by one man in a signal box and signalmen were able to send messages about train times to one another using the telegraph (see page 25). But signals were no use if the train couldn't stop in time. It was not until 1889, after a terrible crash in Armagh, Northern Ireland killed 78 people, that the government forced companies to fit efficient brakes.

**The night mail and night express of the Great Eastern Railway crashed head-on at Thorpe, outside Norwich in 1874. Twenty-two passengers and crew were killed.**

# ARRIVING IN LONDON

**L**aura woke as the train pulled into Maiden Lane station. Two porters carried their heavy trunks to a Hansom cab. The ride to their hotel was slow. The roads were so busy that Laura could only marvel at the crowds. She had never seen so many people earning a living on the streets — and was shocked to see that lots of them were children.

London was not only the largest city in Victorian Britain, it was the largest in the western world. At its core was the old City of London, the Square Mile, and alongside, the City of Westminster, the 'West End'. In 1851 many merchants still lived with their families above their counting houses and the streets were busy with shops, slaughter houses and workshops. But already new suburbs flourished along the tentacles of roads and railways that led to the centre — among them Bayswater and Bethnal Green north of the Thames, and Walworth and Camberwell to the south.

**This drawing *Over London by Rail*, by Gustave Doré, shows the backyards of terraced houses in a slum area of the capital, 1875.**

**A young crossing sweeper touches his forelock as a wealthy lady passes, in this painting by W P Firth, 1855.**

Yet it was not just the size of London that fascinated visitors — it was a city of harsh contrasts. The wealthy lived in elegant Georgian squares, while the teeming slums, the 'rookeries', festered close by. The great city banks loaned money to support the nation's trade with the rest of the world, while abandoned children begged in the streets. Parliament decided the affairs of the empire but the MPs sat behind closed windows to keep out the stink of the black and polluted River Thames.

**To visitors, London seemed full of Hansom cabs – horse-drawn taxis based on a design made in 1834 by Joseph Aloysius Hansom. His 'safety cabs' had large wheels and low slung bodies to reduce injuries to passengers. There were about 4,600 cab drivers in London by 1861 and they had a reputation for being criminals and drunks.**

# THE CRYSTAL PALACE

**T**he next day Laura, her father and governess caught a cab to Hyde Park to visit the Great Exhibition. As they walked through the gates Laura gasped. She had read about the wonderful Crystal Palace but had not realized how beautiful it was. When the sun shone on the glass walls she thought it was like a scene from the *Arabian Nights*. Throngs of visitors were already queuing to enter.

**Raising the ribs of the transept (the main aisle covered by a dome) roof, during the building of the Crystal Palace in December 1850.**

The Great Exhibition was an idea of Prince Albert, the husband of Queen Victoria. He wanted to celebrate the achievements of British and foreign industry. There had been industrial shows before, especially in France, but the Great Exhibition was to be the largest ever held.

The site chosen by the planners was Hyde Park, then on the outskirts of London. Joseph Paxton created a spectacular design for the exhibition building — soon nicknamed the Crystal Palace. Paxton drafted the first sketches on a piece of blotting paper while he was waiting for a train. Only nine days later the full drawings were ready. Brilliantly, his structure was made of

- The Crystal Palace looked like a giant conservatory. It was 610 metres long and 120 metres wide. Some of the trees already growing on the site were left to grow inside.

- There were 1,060 iron columns, supporting 2,224 girders and 358 trusses, forty kilometres of guttering and 300 kilometres of sash bar. The columns were hollow so that they could be used as drain-pipes when it rained.

- After the Great Exhibition the Crystal Palace was taken down and rebuilt at Sydenham Hill in South London. It was eventually destroyed by a fire in 1936.

prefabricated iron and glass. The pieces were made in factories and the building put together on site. Work did not begin until August 1850 but everything was ready for Queen Victoria to open the Great Exhibition on 1 May 1851.

Queen Victoria opens the Great Exhibition on 1 May 1851.

# THE GREAT EXHIBITION

As they walked back to the hotel, Laura and her father discussed the exhibition. 'What did you enjoy most?' he asked. Laura thought hard. 'The Koh-I-Nor diamond from India Papa – and that huge sheet of paper, 2,500 feet long. And the elephant with the howdah. And the knife with eighty blades. And that huge vase from Russia.'

The Great Exhibition of all Nations ran from 1 May to 23 October 1851 and 6,201,856 people paid a visit. For the first three days the entrance fee was £1, expensive enough to ensure the rich had the exhibition to themselves. After this, fees dropped to 1 shilling (5p) from Mondays to Thursdays and ordinary people poured through the gates. Packed excursion trains, run by the railway companies, came from all over the country. Other travellers, like 85-year-old Mary Callinack from Penzance, walked to London!

A cartoon showing an omnibus to the Great Exhibition. So many people wanted to board the buses that they were allowed to sit on the roof – the start of double-decker buses.

**Looking down the central aisle of the Crystal Palace.**

Visitors were not disappointed. There were almost 100,000 objects of all kinds on show. About half were British but others came from as far as Egypt, Morocco, Bolivia, and Persia (Iran). Among the largest items were a steam hammer designed by Henry Nasmyth and the giant hydraulic jacks that had lifted the tubes of the Britannia Railway Bridge between Wales and Anglesey into place.

- The busiest day at the Great Exhibition was 13 October 1851. By 2 pm there were 92,000 visitors on site.

- Messrs Schweppes provided the catering. The best sellers were buns, soda water, lemonade and ginger beers. Ices were made on the spot from a steam powered freezing machine.

- Free public toilets were provided for the first time anywhere.

- The Great Exhibition made a profit of £186,000. The money was used to fund museums and colleges to improve art and design in Britain. These included the Victoria and Albert Museum in South Kensington.

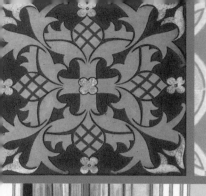

# SENDING A LETTER

**L**ater, Laura wrote a long letter to her mother. She used a pen with a steel nib and a bottle of ink, drying her writing with a sheet of blotting paper. She stuck a penny stamp on the envelope. If the hotel messenger boy hurried to the post office, it would catch the last mail coach and be in her mother's hands in the morning.

The Victorians enjoyed a stunning change in the speed of communications, especially a better postal service. The Post Office had existed for hundreds of years, but the cost of sending a letter depended on how heavy it was and how far it was going. The charges were high and paid by the person who received the letter.

**The General Post Office, London in 1849.**

This picture from 1830 shows how mail was delivered by horse-drawn coach before the days of the train.

In 1840 Rowland Hill set up the 'penny post'. Letters could be sent anywhere for one old penny ($^1/_2$p). To prove they had paid, senders stuck a penny stamp on the envelope.

Most mail was sent by train, in mail coaches, and was sorted on the move. By the 1850s many letters were delivered the next day. By 1867, 642,000,000 letters were sent each year.

- Even quicker than the penny post was the telegraph. Messages were sent as electric signals along wires, often laid next to railway lines. In 1850 a telegraph cable was laid under the English Channel and the first messages were sent between London and Paris. In 1866 a cable 4,160 km long was laid under the Atlantic to Canada.

- William Cooke and Charles Wheatstone invented the telegraph in England in 1837. In 1840 American Samuel Morse invented Morse Code, a quick way of sending messages using a set of long and short signals for every letter of the alphabet.

- In 1876, Alexander Graham Bell, a Scot living in America, invented the telephone — a method of sending speech along wires. By 1879 there were telephone exchanges in London, Liverpool and Manchester.

# A FASHIONABLE RESORT

**T**he next day they caught the train to Brighton. 'We are staying at the queen of seaside resorts, my dear,' said Laura's father. That afternoon he hired a bathing machine for Laura and her governess to take a dip. Later they all dressed in their best clothes and joined the promenade. Everyone was on the seafront to see and be seen!

The most popular holiday for a Victorian family was a trip to the seaside. At first fashionable resorts like Brighton, Weymouth and Scarborough catered for upper- and middle-class visitors who came for a health cure and a refined holiday. By the 1850s ordinary working people were beginning to visit the seaside on cheap train trips.

**The Chain Pier and Marine Parade in Brighton around 1855.**

**A Victorian rhyme about a common peril in seaside hotels.**

I am a bug, a seaside bug,
When folks in bed are lying snug,
About their skin we walk and creep,
And feast upon them while they sleep,
On lodging houses, where we breed
And at this season largely feed.

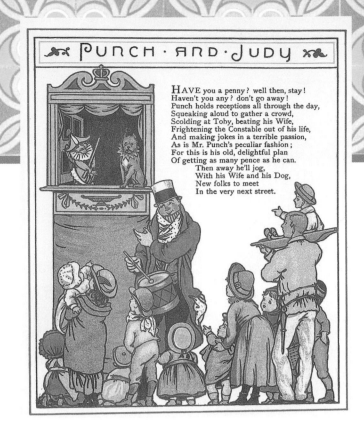

PUNCH · AND · JUDY

HAVE you a penny? well then, stay!
Haven't you any? don't go away!
Punch holds receptions all through the day,
Squeaking aloud to gather a crowd,
Scolding at Toby, beating his Wife,
Frightening the Constable out of his life,
And making jokes in a terrible passion,
As is Mr. Punch's peculiar fashion;
For this is his old, delightful plan
Of getting as many pence as he can.
　　Then away he'll jog,
　　With his Wife and his Dog,
　　New folks to meet
　　In the very next street.

**Punch and Judy shows were always popular with children.**

If the weather was warm, bathing was popular. Wealthier visitors, especially women, hired bathing machines for 1 shilling (5p). They provided a private place to change and were pulled by a horse to the water's edge. No resort was complete without a pier — the longer the better. The Chain Pier in Brighton, built like a suspension bridge, was opened in 1823. But it was soon outclassed by the West Pier, opened in 1866 and stretching 1,115 feet (340 metres) out to sea. Other seaside attractions included promenade concerts, troupes of pierrots (clowns), boat trips, Punch and Judy booths and donkey rides.

**The Prince Regent's Pavilion set the exotic tone of Brighton. In the 1850s it was still a resort where a visitor could hope to see dukes and duchesses and even a prince or two.**

# GOING HOME

**T**he days passed quickly and it was soon time to leave. They took the train to London, but Laura's father had one last treat in store, 'We are going home by steam packet,' he said. They hired a cab to the busy dockside and boarded *The Admiral* – a paddle steamer. 'What a perfect end to our journey,' thought Laura.

Steamboats on the Thames at Gravesend around 1835. In 1821 there were 188 steamers in service on short coastal voyages. By 1853 there were 639, many on ocean routes.

When Victorians proudly sang the patriotic song 'Rule Britannia, Britannia rules the waves,' it wasn't an empty boast. Ever since the Battle of Trafalgar in 1805 the Royal Navy had been unchallenged at sea.

But more importantly, Britain was the leading shipbuilding nation in the world and by 1900 British ships carried almost half of the world's trade.

Ships changed rapidly during Victorian times. In 1837 most were still made of wood and powered by sails. Sensible people thought iron ships would fall apart in a storm or steam engines break down on a long voyage. Then Isambard Kingdom Brunel built two ships that proved them wrong.

The SS *Great Britain* in rough seas. In September 1846 she showed how strong iron ships could be. She ran aground in Dundram Bay, Ireland, and withstood months of storms before being refloated in August 1847.

The first was the *Great Western* — a wooden vessel with a steam engine driving paddle wheels. In 1838 she crossed the Atlantic in 14 days without any problems. His second ship, the *Great Britain* was launched in 1843. She was made of iron and driven by a propeller.

(*Right*) Steam vessels available from London to Newcastle, 1874.

**HERMITAGE STEAM WHARF,**
*Wapping High street,*
J. A. Clinkshill, whartinger.

| Steam Vessels to | Ships | Masters |
|---|---|---|
| EDINBURGH, Leith, Glasgow & Greenock | | |
| One of the following screw steamers of the London & Edinburgh Shipping Company every Wednesday & Saturday, taking passengers & goods for all parts of Scotland. | Marmion . . . . . . . . . .T. Raison<br>Iona . . . . . . . . . .R. C. Hossack<br>Morna . . . . . . . . . .A. Howling<br>Oscar . . . . . . . . . .J. Hutchison<br>Staffa . . . . . . . . . .James Lamb | |

For particulars apply at the Wharf

| NEWCASTLE-ON-TYNE | | |
|---|---|---|
| One of the following screw steamers of the Tyne Steam Shipping Co. every Wednesday & Saturday evening at 6, with passengers & goods for all parts of the north of England. | C. M. Palmer . . . . . . . . . . .Cay<br>Earl Percy . . . . . . . . . .Geddes<br>Grenadier . . . . . . . . . .Newton<br>Admiral . . . . . . . . . . .———— | |

For particulars apply to Alfred T. Bigg, at the Wharf

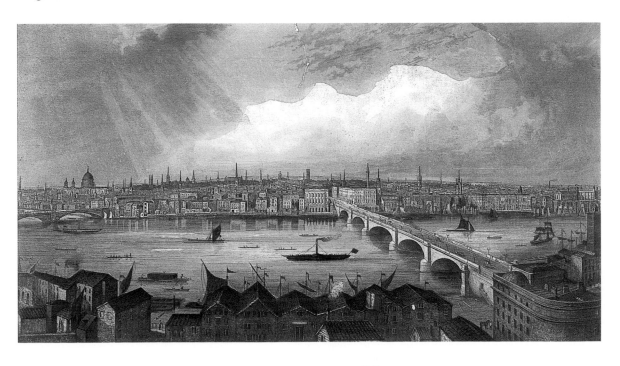

Laura's last view of London was from the busy River Thames.

# TIMELINE

**1837** — On the death of her uncle, William IV, Princess Victoria is crowned queen. Charles Dickens publishes *Oliver Twist*.

**1838** — The London to Birmingham Railway opened.

**1840** — Queen Victoria marries Prince Albert. The Post Master, Rowland Hill, introduces the 'penny post'.

**1842** — The Mines Act bans women and children younger than 10 from working underground.

**1842-6** — The Great Famine in Ireland.

**1844** — Co-op starts in Rochdale.

**1848** — Cholera outbreak kills 53,000 people. First Public Health Act.

**1851** — The Great Exhibition is held at the Crystal Palace in London, to show the wonders of British industry to the world. The census shows more people living in towns than in the country.

**1854** — War with Russia in the Crimea. Florence Nightingale leads a team of nurses.

**1856** — Henry Bessemer's converter halves the cost of steel production.

**1857** — Indians revolt against British rule. The rebellion is ruthlessly crushed.

**1858** — Queen Victoria is crowned Empress of India.

**1859** — Charles Darwin publishes his book on evolution, *On the Origin of Species*.

**1861** — Prince Albert dies from typhoid fever. Queen Victoria begins a lifetime of mourning.

**1865** — The Red Flag Acts cut the speed of 'horseless carriages' to 2 mph in towns.

**1866** — A telegraph cable 2,500 miles (4,160km) long is laid under the Atlantic Ocean.

**1869** — The first Sainsbury's shop opens.

**1870** — School Boards set up to build schools if there is a shortage of places.

**1872** — First FA Cup played – Wanderers 1, Royal Engineers 0.

**1875** — Second Public Health Act. All town councils have to provide a clean water supply and drainage.

**1875** — Captain Webb becomes the first person to swim the English Channel – 40 miles in 22 hours.

**1876** — Alexander Graham Bell invents the telephone.

**1877** — William Booth sets up the Salvation Army in London.

**1882** — Women allowed to keep their own property when they marry.

**1884** — All men who owned or rented houses allowed to vote. Charles Parsons invents the steam turbine.

**1885** — First electric trams run in British cities.

**1887** — Queen Victoria celebrates 50 years as monarch.

**1890** — The Forth Rail Bridge – the longest railway bridge in the world (1,700 feet – 520 m) is opened in Scotland.

**1892** — Keir Hardie elected as MP for West Ham – the first 'Labour Party' MP.

**1899** — Asprin invented.

**1901** — Queen Victoria dies, age 81, on the Isle of Wight. She is succeeded by her son Edward VII.

# GLOSSARY

**Arabian Nights** — Fairy tales from the Middle East.

**ballad** — Song with a story.

**barouche** — A double-seated four-wheeled carriage.

**Britannia Railway Bridge** — Built by Robert Stephenson from Wales to Anglesey. Opened in 1850, the trains ran inside huge iron tubes 30m above the sea.

**carriage people** — A Victorian saying for wealthy and respectable people. Shopkeepers valued customers like this and called them the 'carriage trade'.

**cholera** — A disease that causes terrible sickness and diarrhoea. A person can lose so much water from their bodies that they die.

**class** — Victorian society was deeply divided. People thought of themselves as upper class, middle class or working class.

**counting houses** — Places where businessmen kept their accounts (records to do with money).

**crossing sweeping** — Sweeping the roads so that richer people could cross without getting dirty.

**cutting** — Channel for railway tracks cut through high ground.

**empire** — The lands governed by one country.

**excavation** — Digging.

**gauge** — Width of the railway track.

**gig** — A light two-wheeled carriage.

**girders** — Large iron beams.

**governess** — A private teacher and companion.

**harness** — Equipment fastening the horse to the carriage.

**housemaids** — Servants who cleaned the house.

**howdah** — Seat and canopy on the back of an elephant.

**hydraulic jacks** — Water-powered machines for lifting heavy weights.

**nurserymaids** — Servants who looked after children.

**points** — Switchgear to move trains from one track to another.

**promenade** — A walk taken to look at other people and how they are dressed, also a paved public walk, especially one along a seafront.

**rope works** — A factory for making ropes.

**sash bars** — Iron bars that held the glass in windows.

**signal** — A mechanism to tell the train driver to stop, slow down or carry on.

**specifications** — Plans and measurements.

**steam packet** — Regular steamship service.

**technological** — Using science and industry.

**trusses** — Supports.

**typhoid** — A highly infectious fever that could kill children and adults.

**valet** — A personal servant for a gentleman.

**vendor** — Salesperson.

**viaduct** — A bridge for a railway.

# FURTHER READING

*All About the Industrial Revolution* by Peter Hepplewhite, Hodder Wayland, 2002

*From Workshop to Empire Britain 1750-1900* by Hamish Macdonald, Stanley Thornes, 1995

*The History Detective Investigates: Victorian Transport* by Colin Stott, Hodder Wayland, 2002

# INDEX

DESIGN CHALLENGE

# Super Structures

Keith Good

Evans

# About this book

## About this series

This series involves children in designing and making their own working technology projects, using readily available salvaged or cheap materials. Each project is based on a 'recipe' that promotes success and crucially, stimulates the reader's own ideas. The 'recipes' also provide a good introduction to important technology in everyday life. The projects can be developed to different levels of sophistication according to the reader's ability and can reflect their other interests. The series teaches skills and knowledge in a fun way and encourages creative, innovative ideas.

## About this book

Understanding structures matters because they are such an important part of our world. Our skeletons are natural structures, so are shells, spiders' webs and plant stems. People design and make a huge variety of structures to live in, sit on, walk over, carry things or rely on in other ways. Despite their variety, all structures have to be able to stand up to the forces and loads that they will encounter. Through design projects in this book, children discover that some shapes are much stronger than others and how this can save resources. Practical activities in this book give an understanding of structures and how materials behave when different forces act on them. This relates to the Science curriculum e.g. 'compare everyday materials....relate these properties to everyday uses' and 'forces'. Designing stable structures that don't fall over, balancing forces to keep things up and the main kinds of bridges are also covered through activities. Structures that are rigid but can collapse when we want them to (like baby buggies) are important in everyday life and this idea is used as a basis for several design projects. Well designed structures use materials economically. A packaging project raises this issue and encourages wise use of materials. As in every book in this series, the reader is encouraged to get real understanding through marrying 'recipes' and knowledge with their own ideas and imagination.

## Safety

● A small screwdriver or awl can be used to make holes but the corrugated card must be supported by a slab of modelling clay or thick card – not a hand. Protect work surfaces with a piece of board.

● If a structure is to be tested to destruction (until it gives way), make it from weak materials like the ones suggested in this book, otherwise dangerous amounts of weight may be needed.

● Adult use of craft knives is strongly advised. These must be used with a cutting board (or mat) and a safety rule with a groove to protect the fingers. Card is often best cut for children on a paper trimmer with a guarded wheel cutter.

# Contents

# Materials and forces

## Testing the strength of materials

All designers (including you) need to choose the right materials for their projects. This means knowing about different forces and how materials behave. Structures have to cope with *static* forces like their own weight and *dynamic* forces like wind. When standing on scales you cause a static force. When you jump on the scales you cause a bigger dynamic force. If we know what kinds of force will work on a structure it helps us to choose materials that will cope. Paper is very strong when pulled (*tension*) but very weak when twisted (*torsion*). Stone and brick are strongest when being squashed (*compression*) but will not bend without breaking. Try these experiments to find out how some materials behave.

## You will need

- strips of paper
- thin card
- 30cm plastic ruler
- twig or used match
- elastic band
- modelling clay
- string
- piece of fabric

## Bending

1. Take a twig or used match and watch closely as you bend it until it breaks. What happened to the top surface? What happened to the bottom surface?

2. Hold a strip of paper tightly on each side of a plastic ruler. Bend the ruler upwards then downwards. Notice when the strips stretch and squash.

3. Put cuts into both sides of a block of modelling clay and bend it. Which surface is stretched (in tension) and which surface is squashed (in compression)?

**1**

twig

**2**

paper

30cm plastic ruler

**3**

modelling clay

## Twisting

Try twisting a strip of paper, modelling clay, string or fabric. Notice how each material behaves.

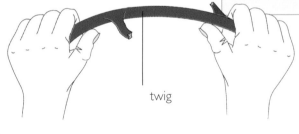

## Stretching

Try stretching modelling clay, a twig, an elastic band, a strip of paper, a piece of fabric and string. Which resist stretching best? Materials like wire are good at coping with tension.

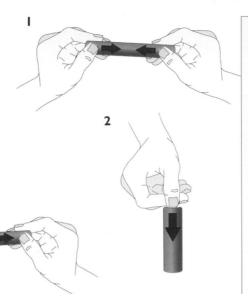

## Squashing

1. Take a twig and push inwards from each end. Is a short twig stiffer than a long one of the same thickness? How do a strip of paper and piece of string or fabric behave?

2. Make a cylinder of modelling clay and compress (squash) it. It is not brittle and won't break but watch closely how it behaves.

## Shear force

Shear forces try to make one part of a structure slide past another.

Shearing happens when scissors cut paper or cloth.

1. Use a hole punch, paper strip and a modelling clay pin to see a shearing force at work. Metal bolts often have to cope with shear forces.

2. Compare paper strips joined by a paper fastener with strips that have been glued and left to dry. Which is best at coping with a pull?

Making holes for bolts and other fixings can cause weakness – this is why many aircraft parts are just glued!

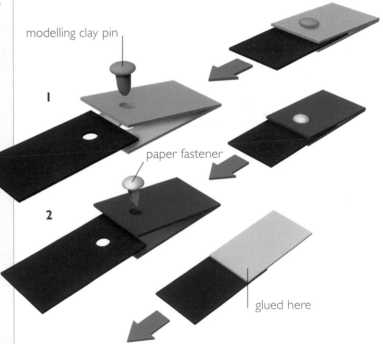

modelling clay pin

paper fastener

glued here

## Getting ideas

Design a way to record what happens when you try the activities on these pages. Drawings, charts, lists and perhaps a computer could help you to show your results. Can you collect other materials to try? Make a poster showing bad or silly uses for different materials, like using cheese to make a ladder, polystyrene for a tightrope or string to push something. You could collect and display different materials and pictures of them in use. Think about why different products use different materials. You could separate natural materials like wood and wool from ones made by people, like plastic.

# Beams
## Making strong shapes

Lots of things that you see every day are shaped to make them strong. Careful shaping saves weight and money, and avoids wasting material. Some food tins and sandwich packaging have ridges to make them strong. Why do you think baby buggies are made from tubes instead of solid bars?

A piece of material that has to resist bending is called a beam. The shape of a beam affects how stiff it is and the load it can carry. Here is a chance to find out about beams for yourself.

**Some beam shapes to try**

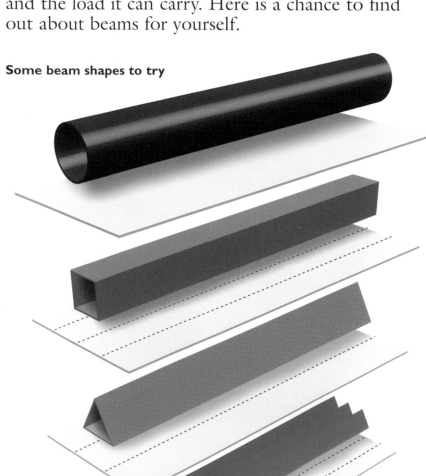

## You will need

- Some pieces of A4 paper (use scrap paper if you can) cut in half lengthways
- Sticky tape (masking tape is best)
- Weights e.g. standard metal ones, plasticine blocks of the same weight or a bag of marbles
- 2 piles of books or another way of making a gap for testing your beams

**Tip**
A worn out ball-point pen, and a ruler are useful for making creases.

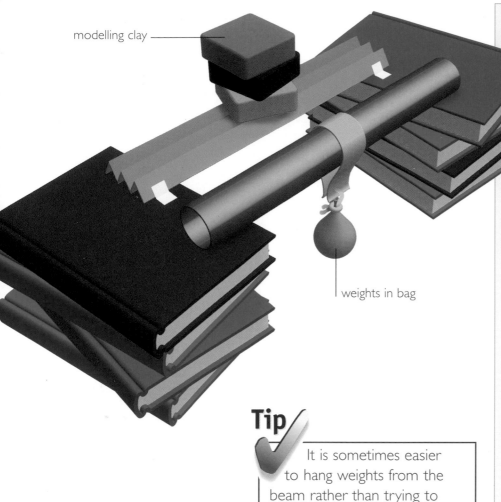

modelling clay

weights in bag

## What to do

1. Make the beams shown on page 8, using sticky tape to hold the beams in shape.

2. Arrange your books with a gap of 22cm so that you can test your beams.

3. Try bridging the gap with a flat piece of paper first. Next, test the beams you have made, using enough tape to hold them in shape.

4. Add weight to the middle of your beam a little at a time. **Safety**: don't use weights that are easily broken or heavy and dangerous!

5. Record the shape of each beam and the weight it carried before collapsing.

## Tip ✓

It is sometimes easier to hang weights from the beam rather than trying to balance them on top.

## Getting ideas

Try out your own beam ideas. Could you combine some of the shapes to make a new idea? Remember, always start with the same sized paper for a fair test.

Can you think of other ways to support a beam?

Look for strong shapes in buildings, sports and play equipment and many other things around you. You could record these with notes and drawings.

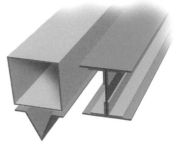

# Strong shapes
## Triangles and shells

There are two main kinds of structure. Frame structures are made up from pieces which are joined together. Triangles are rigid shapes so they are often used to make strong but light frames. You can see triangles at work in building-site cranes, bridges, bicycle frames and kites. Shell or *monocoque* structures allow thin material to be made much more rigid by forming it into 'shells'. Seashells, eggs and beetle wing covers are examples in the natural world. Domes, egg boxes, plastic bowls, polystyrene food trays and clear plastic bubble packs are examples of shell structures made by people. Try making the shapes on these pages and test their strength.

## You will need

- strips of corrugated cardboard (the 'tubes' in the cardboard should run *along* the strips)
- paper fasteners
- 6 sticks or pieces of wooden dowel rod about 30cm long
- elastic bands
- white glue
- clear plastic bubble pack

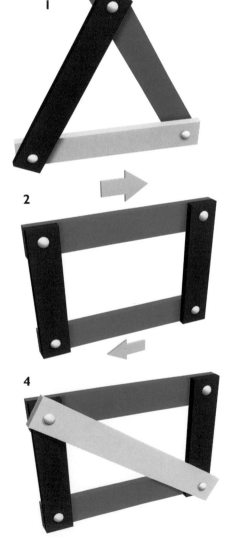

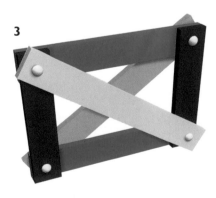

## What to do

1. Make a triangular frame using paper fasteners and strips of corrugated cardboard. Notice how rigid the triangle is.

2. Make a rectangular frame and notice how easily it collapses.

3. Now fix two strips across the frame. This is called *triangulation*. Notice how rigid the structure has become.

4. Remove one of the cross pieces and notice that the frame is still rigid. Part of a structure that can be taken away without weakening it is called a *redundant member*.

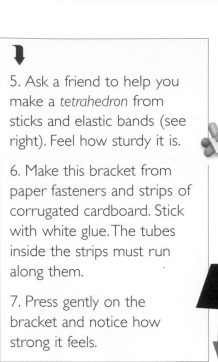

**5**

**tetrahedron**

5. Ask a friend to help you make a *tetrahedron* from sticks and elastic bands (see right). Feel how sturdy it is.

6. Make this bracket from paper fasteners and strips of corrugated cardboard. Stick with white glue. The tubes inside the strips must run along them.

7. Press gently on the bracket and notice how strong it feels.

**6**

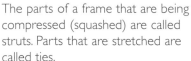

tie

strut

The parts of a frame that are being compressed (squashed) are called struts. Parts that are stretched are called ties.

A triangle makes this bracket rigid. The strut becomes a tie when the bracket is turned upside down.

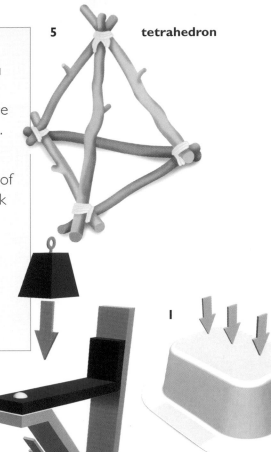

**I**

**2**

# What to do

Bubble packs are strong shell structures. The shape makes the pack much stronger than a flat sheet.

1. Cup your hand over a bubble pack and press down steadily to feel how strong the structure is.

2. Cut off the flat base to see if this makes any difference to the strength.

To make a special shell structure, see page 20.

## Getting ideas

Think of uses for your tetrahedron. Could it be a shelter, a model of play equipment or something else? Could a number of these structures be put together to do useful jobs?

Design uses for the bracket you have made. You could make one or two more and use them to support a small shelf. Make the shelf from corrugated cardboard, taking care that tubes inside run *along* the shelf.

Collect clear bubble pack shell structures. Can you recycle them as the covers for hand-held games that you design? Small balls or cut-out shapes could be steered or tapped into parts of the playing surface. The clear shell lets players see but stops them touching the pieces.

# Stable structures
## Testing shapes on a test ramp

It is often very important that structures don't tip over in use. A *stable* structure does not tip over easily. An *unstable* structure will tip over easily. People are not very stable structures. When you stand and lean forwards a little you can feel how unstable you are.

The activities here will help you to understand why some things fall over more easily than others. This knowledge should help you design your own stable structures.

## You will need

- corrugated cardboard
- A4 card
- paper
- masking tape or clear tape
- modelling clay
- drinking straws
- small cardboard box or tube
- cork
- 2 kebab sticks

## What to do

How to make a test ramp. You can share this with one or more friends.

1. Cut a piece of A4 card in half and join the pieces at the end with tape to make a hinge.

2. Stick a strip of corrugated cardboard across the ramp.

3. Fix some paper to a piece of cardboard. Use modelling clay to make some of the shapes shown.

4. Put your shapes against the strip of card and tilt the ramp very slowly. On the paper, mark the angle when the shapes topple. Number the shapes and angle lines.

5. Design your own stable and unstable shapes and try them on your ramp. You could also try other things that won't break.

Do you notice anything about the most stable shapes? Do the least stable shapes have anything in common?

Work out a way to record your results. Show at what angle each shape fell. You could use a computer to help you show your results.

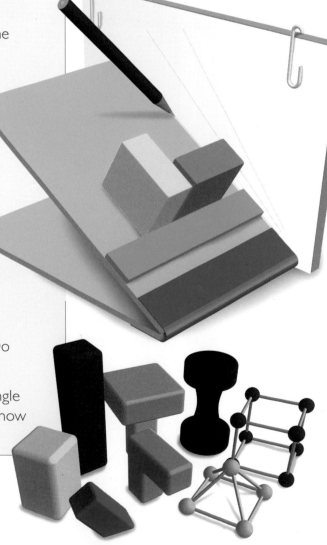

# What to do

You might think you can tell how stable a shape is by the way it looks – but you can't always.

1. Tape a modelling clay weight near the top of a small cardboard box or tube. What else could you use as a weight?

2. Try the box or tube on your test ramp. First put the weight at the top, then put it at the bottom. Which way up is the most stable?

Look at cantilevers on page 14.

modelling clay

Here's how to make a very stable balancing structure using kebab sticks, a cork and some modelling clay.

cork

kebab stick

**Tip**

A plastic bottle full of water makes a good place to stand your 'balancer'.

plastic bottle

modelling clay

How does raising or lowering the arms affect the stability? Would longer or shorter arms or base make a difference?

## Getting ideas

Make design drawings for a very stable vehicle that would be difficult to turn over. Make design drawings for a new kind of wheeled vehicle to carry a baby and shopping. Could your design carry a toddler too? **Important**: think about where the weight will go so that your design would not tip over. You could model your designs, using a construction kit or other materials and clay weights.

**Balancer** Try using your stable balancer as part of a design for a game. Could you balance things on the balancer? You could word-process a set of rules.

# Equilibrium
## Balancing forces to keep things up

When two tug-of-war teams pull with the same amount of force they stay still because their pulling forces *balance* or are *in equilibrium*. If two people of the same weight sit on the ends of a see-saw it will balance. Balanced pulling (tension) from different directions can be used to keep things in place. Radio masts, sailing ship masts, metal chimneys and tents are all held up by balancing the pull of cables or ropes.

Here are some ideas for making structures by balancing forces or getting them in equilibrium. If the forces don't balance, your structures will fall!

## What to do

1. Balance a ruler over the edge of a table. Put modelling clay or another small weight on the table end.

2. Put the same amount of weight on the unsupported end of the ruler. How far out can the ruler extend (stick out) without the structure falling?

3. Try adding extra weights to the table end. Each time you add a weight, see how much further the ruler can extend.

How far can a structure that is balanced in the middle be built out on each side? Structures like this are based on balanced cantilevers – a cantilever is a beam that sticks out from its support. Experiment, using toy wooden blocks.

## You will need

- 30cm ruler
- modelling clay (or small weights)
- rectangular wooden blocks
- paper kitchen towels
- thread
- drinking straw or kebab sticks
- masking tape
- corrugated cardboard
- sheet of A4 paper

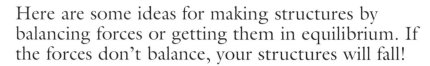

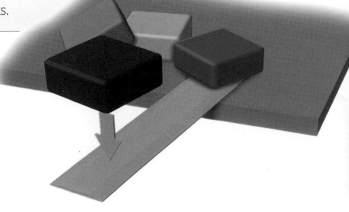

# Making a mast

Using only one sheet of A4 paper, and a small amount of masking tape, see how tall a radio mast you can build.

1. Make a base for your mast from a piece of corrugated cardboard.

2. Make stiff shapes from the paper to build your mast (see page 8).

3. Use ties or guy ropes made from thread and fixed with tape to help you support a really tall mast.

# Making a tent

Balance the pulling forces on the guy ropes to support tents and shelters.

1. Make a base for your tent from a piece of corrugated cardboard.

2. Try making a tent like the one shown. Use kitchen towel, and straws or kebab sticks, thread and tape. Make the tent as sturdy as possible.

## Getting ideas

Tent structures are used as shelters when fishing or camping, and to keep the sun off. They can also be used to protect explorers and to house people after a disaster. Structures like this are easy to fold down into a small space and are quite light to move about. Design and make your own tent structures. You could design a structure with more than one 'room'. Your structure could be for a special purpose. Think about other structures that could be held up by balanced forces. Could you design a hammock supported by poles and ropes? Look in catalogues to see what other people have designed.

# Bridges
## Bridging gaps with strength and stability

Bridges are important structures. They make journeys shorter, safer and easier. Bridges have to be light so that they do not sag under their own weight or waste materials and resources. They have to be as strong as possible so that they can carry heavy loads. There are four basic kinds of bridge: beam, cantilever, arch and suspension bridge. Find out about bridges by making these.

## Beam bridges

Beam bridges can be single span (one beam) or multi-span (several beams).

Frameworks called trusses are often used to make bridges that are strong but light.

thin card

paper triangles

The deck of the bridge rests on top of the framework base

6 cm

6 cm

**plan**

## You will need

- paper artstraws or dried spaghetti
- thin card and paper
- modelling clay
- corrugated cardboard
- string
- masking tape
  - heavy books

## What to do

Make your own bridges using artstraws or sphaghetti to bridge a 20cm gap, perhaps between a pile of books.

1. Draw the plan on this page full size and build your bridge sides on it. Hold parts still with masking tape while you glue the paper triangles.

2. Turn the frame over carefully and glue triangles on the other side.

3. Let the sides of your bridge dry before joining them to each other. Don't use too much glue and let it dry well. Glue on a thin card deck (like a roadway) to hold the load.

4. Add a little weight at a time to see how much your bridge can carry. Try different designs and compare yours with others made by friends.

Here are other truss designs. Design your own too. Make full-sized plans.

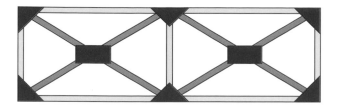

## Cantilever bridges

Cantilever bridges are made up of beams that are only supported at one end. Trap one end of a ruler between heavy books to make a quick cantilever. Often two cantilevers (see page 14) are used with a short beam between them. The Forth Railway Bridge in Scotland is one example.

## Lifting bridges

Lifting bridges are supported at one end so that they can be raised to let ships pass. Tower Bridge in London is one example.

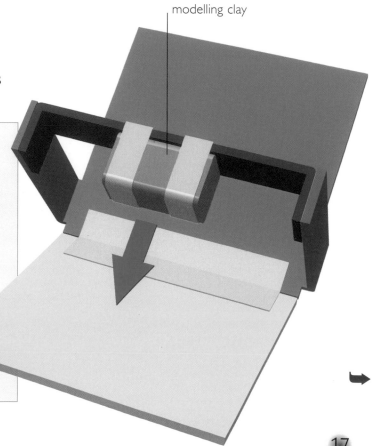

modelling clay

### **What to do**

Make a lifting bridge like this from corrugated cardboard.

1. Notice that adding a weight (a *counter weight*) fixed high up makes the bridge very easy to raise. This saves energy and might make it possible for just one person raise and lower a bridge.

2. Try different amounts of weight. Can you add too much? What would happen if the arch was taller?

## Arch bridges

The Romans found that wedge-shaped stones called *voussoirs* could carry heavy loads when built into an arch. Look out for arches in buildings as well as bridges. Materials that stand up well to compression (squashing), like stone and brick, are used. Modern arches are often made from reinforced concrete. Arches are built over a support that is taken away once the last piece, the middle or keystone, is in place. Strong support is needed at the ends of the arch to stop it spreading outwards.

**1**

**2**

keystone

**template**

20°

thin card support

**Tip** You can make your arch bigger by enlarging this template, using a photocopier or computer.

## What to do

1. Lay a thin sheet of card between two heavy books. Gradually add weights to see how much it will carry.

2. Now make the card into an arch and see how much more weight it will take. Is a high arch stronger or weaker than a low one?

To make an arch that will be strong although the pieces are not fixed together:

1. Trace off the template below and use it to make an arch in modelling clay.

2. Cut the arch into the nine voussoirs with a table knife. Build the arch between heavy books on a thin card support.

3. Once the arch is complete, carefully take away the support. Press down gradually to feel how strong an arch can be.

You could go on to try higher and lower arches.

# Suspension bridges

Suspension bridges can reach across (or *span*) large distances without using lots of material. In jungle areas they are sometimes made from creepers and bamboo. Suspension bridges carrying roads rely on strong steel cables in tension (being pulled). The pulling forces on one cable are in equilibrium, one force is balanced by another (see page 14). Wind can be a danger to suspension bridges and they have to be designed to cope with it.

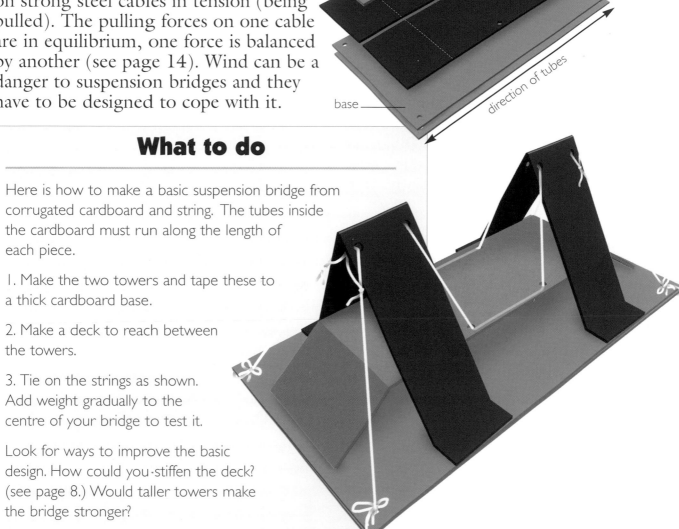

deck

tower

base

direction of tubes

## What to do

Here is how to make a basic suspension bridge from corrugated cardboard and string. The tubes inside the cardboard must run along the length of each piece.

1. Make the two towers and tape these to a thick cardboard base.

2. Make a deck to reach between the towers.

3. Tie on the strings as shown. Add weight gradually to the centre of your bridge to test it.

Look for ways to improve the basic design. How could you stiffen the deck? (see page 8.) Would taller towers make the bridge stronger?

## Getting ideas

Find out more about bridges by looking in books and perhaps using a CD-ROM. Where are there famous bridges and which is the longest? Make a display about bridges and collect pictures of them. Try to sort them into different kinds e.g. beam, cantilever, arch and suspension bridges. You could add your own bridges and information about your tests. How many stories, songs or poems about bridges can you find? Perhaps you could write some?

Imagine what would happen if all the bridges vanished. Look at and draw or photograph bridges in your area.

# Domes

## Exploring rounded shapes

Domes were first built long ago and they are found in many countries. They vary in shape when seen from the side but they are all circular when seen from above. Domes have been made from clay, wooden poles thatched with palms, fabric, metal, concrete and even snow. A dome is a kind of shell structure (page 10). A dome can enclose a large space using less material than other structures, and rounded shapes are often stronger than flat ones. If you were to cut a slice from the middle of a dome, you would have made an arch (page 18), which is a strong shape when pressed under weight.

Try making these dome structures to see how strong they can be.

press down

### Tip

If you scoop out the inside of half an orange or grapefruit you have also made a dome.

## You will need

- plastic bottle
- clear tape
- corrugated cardboard
- round balloon
- newspaper
- flour and water

## What to do

1. With adult help, cut the top from a plastic bottle to make a dome.

2. Press down on the top to feel what a strong shape a dome is. Squeeze from the side and the dome feels much weaker.

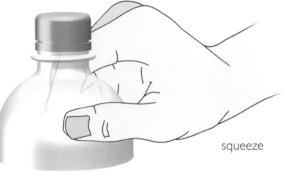

squeeze

## What to do

To make a dome using a balloon as a *former*.

1. Wear an apron and cover your working area with plastic sheet.

2. Cut a circular hole in a piece of corrugated cardboard to hold the balloon.

3. Blow up the balloon so that it fits snugly in the hole and tie the neck. Support the bottom of the balloon in a box or bowl.

4. Mix flour with a little water at a time to make a creamy paste. Tear strips of newspaper about 2cm wide.

4. Brush the strips with the paste, and lay them over the balloon and base. Continue adding strips until you have a layer about 3mm thick.

5. Leave in a warm place to dry well while you work on the ideas below. When dry, pop the balloon and you have a dome!

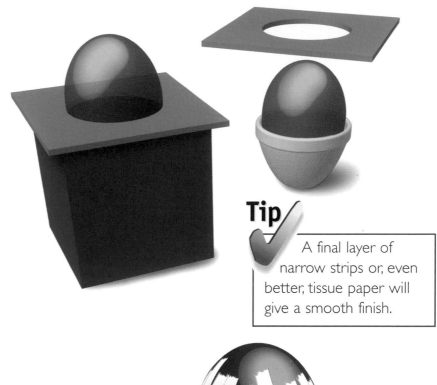

**Tip**

A final layer of narrow strips or, even better, tissue paper will give a smooth finish.

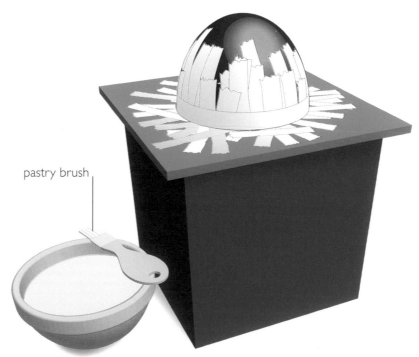

pastry brush

### Getting ideas

Your dome could be part of a design for a building of the future or even part of a city or village of the future. You could model the outside of the building and its surroundings and draw what it is like inside. You could go on to model the inside too. What will the building be for? How could you make your building kind to the environment? Where would the building be built? It could be in a desert, under the sea or even on another planet. Look at homes from different times, countries and climates.

Look for domes near where you live or in books and on CD-ROM.

# Structures that collapse

Designing structures that fold flat

We can design structures that are strong and rigid but collapse and fold flat when we want them to. This saves a lot of space and makes the products easier to transport. Collapsible structures are all around us; they include folding pushchairs, ironing boards, tent frames and camping or picnic furniture. Blow-up water toys, swimming armbands and even armchairs can be collapsed by letting the air out. Can you think of more things that can be collapsed? Fold-flat furniture would allow a hall or room to be cleared for games or dancing. Lots of flattened shelters could fit into one rescue aircraft. Try out some collapsible structures, think of uses for them and perhaps design your own. Read page 23 for some ideas to help you.

## You will need

- corrugated cardboard to make the structures
- brown paper tape or thin card
- thin card or paper

## What to do

1. Look at the picture at the bottom. The arrow shows the way the tubes in the corrugated cardboard go. Mark yours out so that the tubes run the same way.

2. Cut out the pieces you need from strips that are about 8cm wide. Mark out the shapes to look like the pictures.

3. Make the creases or joins and put your structures together. To make sharp creases in the right place press down on the line with a ruler and lift the corrugated cardboard to bend it.

4. Press gently on your structures from different directions. Do they feel weaker when pressed some ways compared with others?

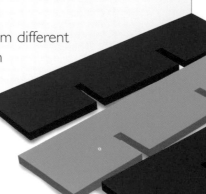

The slots lock together like this

direction of tubes

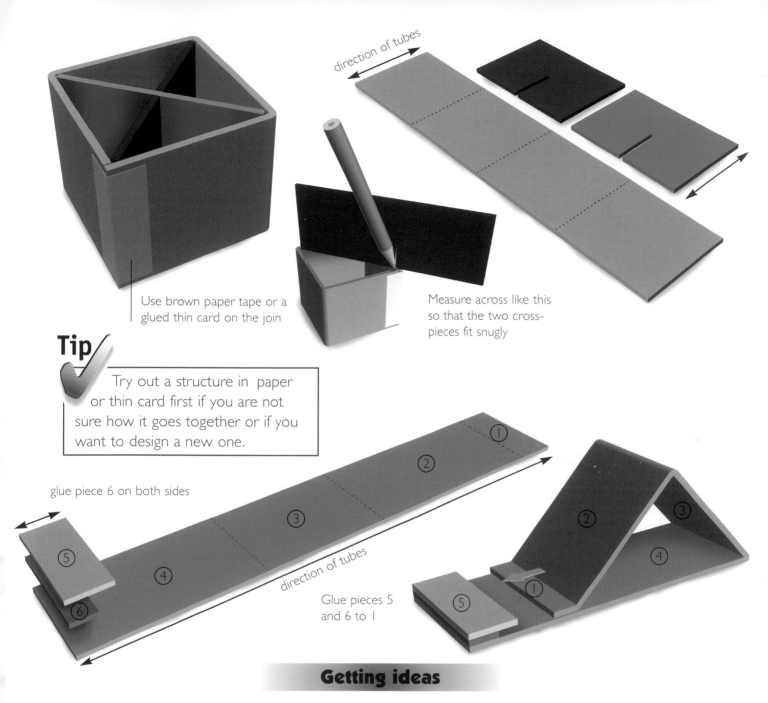

direction of tubes

Use brown paper tape or a glued thin card on the join

Measure across like this so that the two cross-pieces fit snugly

**Tip**

Try out a structure in paper or thin card first if you are not sure how it goes together or if you want to design a new one.

glue piece 6 on both sides

① ② ③ ④ ⑤ ⑥

direction of tubes

Glue pieces 5 and 6 to 1

② ③ ④ ⑤ ①

## Getting ideas

Look at the structures you have made. Turn them different ways up. What could they be used for? Could they store or hold something? Could you design a gift that would be easy to post to someone? Could you design games that use the structures? What could go in the holes: pencils, marbles or something else? You could paint or decorate your finished object. You could design a display stand for one of your favourite things. Look for fold-flat corrugated cardboard display stands in shops. Imagine that your structures were much bigger and perhaps made from something else. Draw some ideas for using bigger collapsible structures. Ideas could include furniture, survival shelters or something for the beach. Could you draw fold-flat ideas to help someone who could not find a spare seat on a train?

# Pop-ups
## Structures that seem to vanish!

Some structures can fold flat then almost put *themselves* up. Children's play tents and tunnels can pop up when taken out of their bag. Life rafts are inflated by gas cylinders and some life vests blow up automatically when a person falls in the water. Some greetings cards pop up when they are taken out of their envelope. Pop-ups are often used in books to make things look realistic. They are also used in advertising. Try making these structures that pop up when a folded card is opened.

## You will need

- coloured card A4 size
- colouring equipment

## What to do

To make each pop-up:

1. Cut a piece of A4 card in half and fold one piece in two to make a base.

2. Draw the *net* of the pop-up carefully on the other piece. Cut the solid lines and score on the dotted ones.

3. Make your pop-ups look like the ones in the pictures. Glue any tabs — don't use too much.

4. Fold the base card and the pop-up should vanish inside.

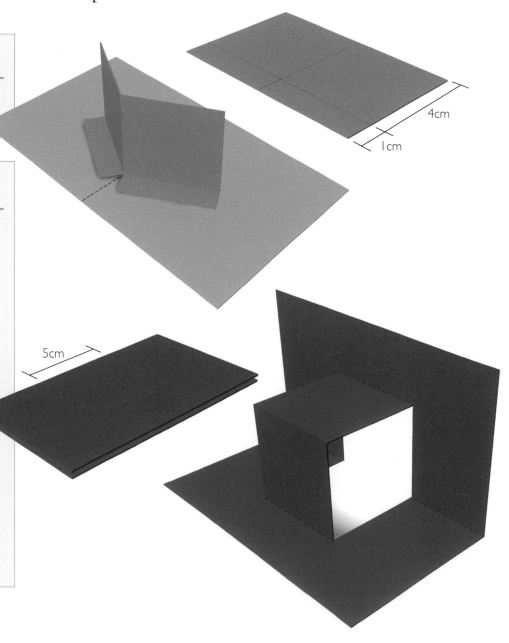

4cm

1cm

5cm

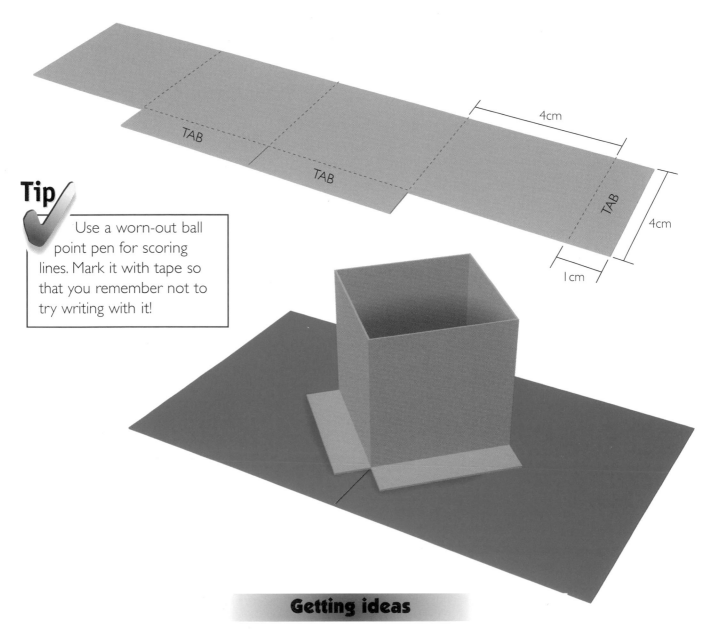

4cm

4cm

1cm

TAB

TAB

TAB

**Tip**

Use a worn-out ball point pen for scoring lines. Mark it with tape so that you remember not to try writing with it!

## Getting ideas

What could you use your pop-ups for? Turn the pop-ups and look at them from different angles to get ideas. You could put more than one pop-up on each folding base. Try making your pop-ups into greetings cards or games. Perhaps you could design a greetings card that is also a game! Could games pieces be thrown into a pop-up, rolled at it or fished out of it? Do holes or slots need to be cut? You also need to think about the age of the user and the kind of rules they could understand.

Use computer word-processing and graphics if you can.

Imagine that your the pop-ups were much bigger and draw your ideas. You would need to use corrugated cardboard if you went on to make big pop-ups. What could large pop-ups be used for? Could the last pop-up (above) be used to make furniture or a play house if it was big enough? Look for examples of pop-up structures and try to see how they work.

# Structures that protect
## Designing packaging for fragile objects

Natural structures that give protection include seed cases, nuts, crab shells and egg shells. Your skull does the important job of protecting your brain. People make structures to protect our bodies, food and other things. Can you think of things that are packaged to protect them? Protection can be springy like plastic bubble wrap and foam, or rigid like plastic or metal. Protective packaging allows fragile things to be transported or posted without damage. Like other well-designed structures, a good package uses as little material as possible to do the job. This saves weight and money, and is kind to our environment.

See what super structures you can design to protect fragile objects.

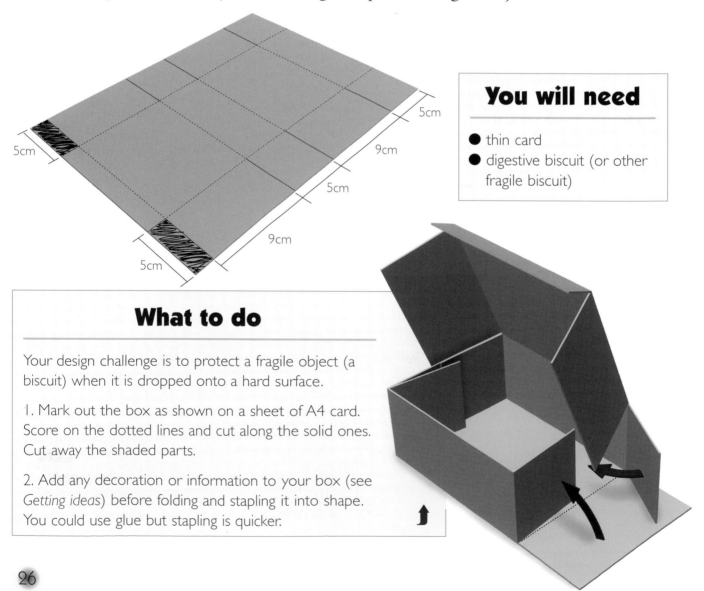

## You will need

- thin card
- digestive biscuit (or other fragile biscuit)

## What to do

Your design challenge is to protect a fragile object (a biscuit) when it is dropped onto a hard surface.

1. Mark out the box as shown on a sheet of A4 card. Score on the dotted lines and cut along the solid ones. Cut away the shaded parts.

2. Add any decoration or information to your box (see *Getting ideas*) before folding and stapling it into shape. You could use glue but stapling is quicker.

3. Explore things that could go in your box to protect the biscuit (see pages 6–9). Make your protection ideas and fit them in with the biscuit.

4. Hold the box closed with a little masking tape so that you can open it easily later.

5. Starting quite low, drop the box *bottom down* onto a hard surface like concrete. Drop five times then check for damage. If the biscuit survives, gradually increase the height you drop from.

**Safety**: you could stand on a chair but for any greater heights you *must* get adult help.

**Tip** Remember that broken biscuits are not wasted they can still be eaten or put on a bird table!

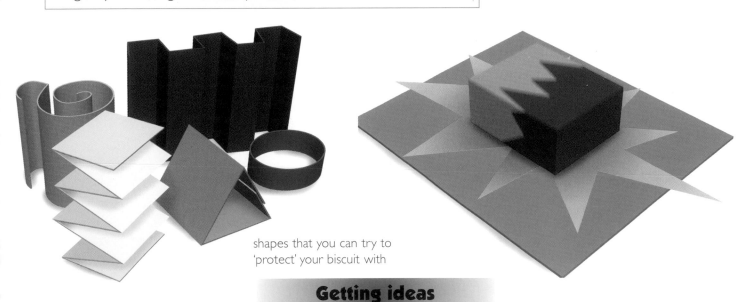

shapes that you can try to 'protect' your biscuit with

## Getting ideas

Here are some more things to try. You could just draw your ideas or go on to make and try them. Try protecting the biscuit using a range of salvaged materials. Imagine the package is to be delivered by post – keep it as light as you can to keep the price of postage low. Play around with ideas for delivering the biscuit safely. Could a parachute be used, or a slide? Sometimes crazy ideas turn out to be useful. Can you think of other ways to test a package? Could you design something using elastic bands to launch a package against a wall? How could you measure how much force was being used each time? Cars with dummies inside are crash-tested to see how safe they will be for real people. You could draw or model a car that you think would protect the passengers really well. Collect packaging and look at it closely. Packaging is often used to make people want to buy what is inside as well as protecting it, and it may also give instructions. You could design a package like this to help sell a product that you have made up.

# Containers

## Resisting forces from inside

Natural containers include eggs, nests, seashells and kangaroos' pouches. People have made containers from many different materials including clay, fabric, glass, wood, card and steel. Containers are used to hold, store, protect and carry all sorts of things. Sacks, nets, cans, buckets and bowls are just a few examples of containers that have to cope with forces from inside.

Thousands of paper bags are used every day to hold and carry things. See if you can design and make a strong, long-lasting, useful and attractive paper bag. Before you make your finished bag, make a *prototype* to try out your ideas.

## You will need

- sheet of A3 paper
- materials like card, string and plastic that could be used to make bag handles
- corrugated cardboard to make dividers

5cm

12cm

8cm

12cm

8cm

crease and fold along dashed lines, cut along the solid lines

## What to do

1. Follow the pictures to measure, cut and fold the basic prototype bag. Stick with white glue and leave to dry well.

2. Read the first part of 'getting ideas', then design handles for your bag.

**Tip**

You could use a stapler as well as glue to fix handles.

3. Hang your bag up and gradually load it with weights like oranges or blocks of modelling clay to see how it copes.

You could make more than one bag and try different ideas for handles or compare your ideas with handles made by your friends.

Once you have made a strong prototype bag that is comfortable to carry, you could use what you have learned to make a finished project. Just one person's idea is shown. What will yours be like?

Think about what will go in your bag. Would carton dividers keep the contents in good condition or make them easier to find?

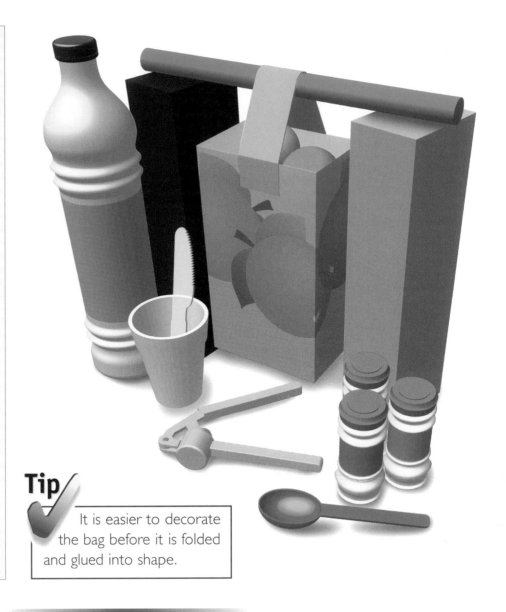

**Tip** ✔ It is easier to decorate the bag before it is folded and glued into shape.

## Getting ideas

Bags are used for lots of different things. Handles make bags easier to carry. Look at handles on rucksacks, sports bags, carrier bags and others you can find. What could you use to make bag handles that are strong and comfortable? How will you join them to the bag? Does the bag need to be made stronger where handles are fixed? How could you do this? Can you make other parts of the bag stronger?

What will your bag be used for? You could add dividers to make different layers. Sweet things might be needed last at a picnic and could go on the bottom. Could you make a structure to stop them being squashed? Would pockets make things easier to find? Does the bag need to be kept closed? How could you do this if it did? You could decorate your bag with paints, perhaps by printing with a carved potato (get adult help) or by sticking things on. Can you think of other ways to improving the basic bag design?

# Index